To [illegible] ees

(Writer in residence, North Lodge Park, Darlington,
July 2004 - December, 2005)

'And this our life, exempt from public haunt,
Finds tongues in trees, books in the running brooks,
Sermons in stones, and good in everything.
I would not change it.'
William Shakespeare, *As You Like It*

New Writing North

First Published in 2005 by
New Writing North
2 School Lane
Whickham
Newcastle upon Tyne
NE16 4SL
www.newwritingnorth.com

New Writing North Limited 3166037
Registered Charity Number 1062729

ISBN 0-9541456-8-2

Typesetting and design: John Adair
Cover photo: David Williams
Printed by Aero Printing

For the community of North Lodge Park

'Trees are poems that earth writes upon the sky.
We fell them down and turn them into paper
that we may record our emptiness'
Kahlil Gibran

Acknowledgements

Thanks are due to Darlington Borough Council, (in particular to Wendy Scott and Kari Vickers), to New Writing North, (in particular Claire Malcolm and Anna Summerford), to the photographer, David Williams, and to sculptor Andrew McKeown.

A special thanks to Peter Sherry (Arboricultural Officer), and to Yvonne Richardson, who walked with me round the condemned trees.

This project was supported by:

The Big Lottery Fund
The Children's Fund
Early Years, Darlington Borough Council
SureStart

Introduction

This little chapbook is not the main outcome of my writer's residency, but is a special dedication in memory of the trees condemned during the period of that residency. I always think it's sad when trees have to be felled, some people say they scream when they are chopped down - I don't know. What I do know is that I felt compelled to try and make them live on in some way and as a writer, this seemed the best way.

The main book of poems and writing by the community and my acknowledgement to many more individuals will be published in 2006, along with a separate publication, which documents the project and will feature text and photographs.

I remember going round the park with Peter Sherry, (who was the Borough Arboricultural Officer at the time) and with Yvonne Richardson, Chair of The Friends. It was as if we were paying our final respects. Peter gave me a map of the condemned trees. The large number shocked me.

I am donating these poems. The proceeds from the sale of this book will be handed to The Friends of North Lodge Park so that they can purchase replacement trees - it's my way of saying a very personal thank you for allowing me into your community and of giving you something back.

Maureen Almond
Writer in residence, North Lodge Park, Darlington
(July 2004 - December 2005)

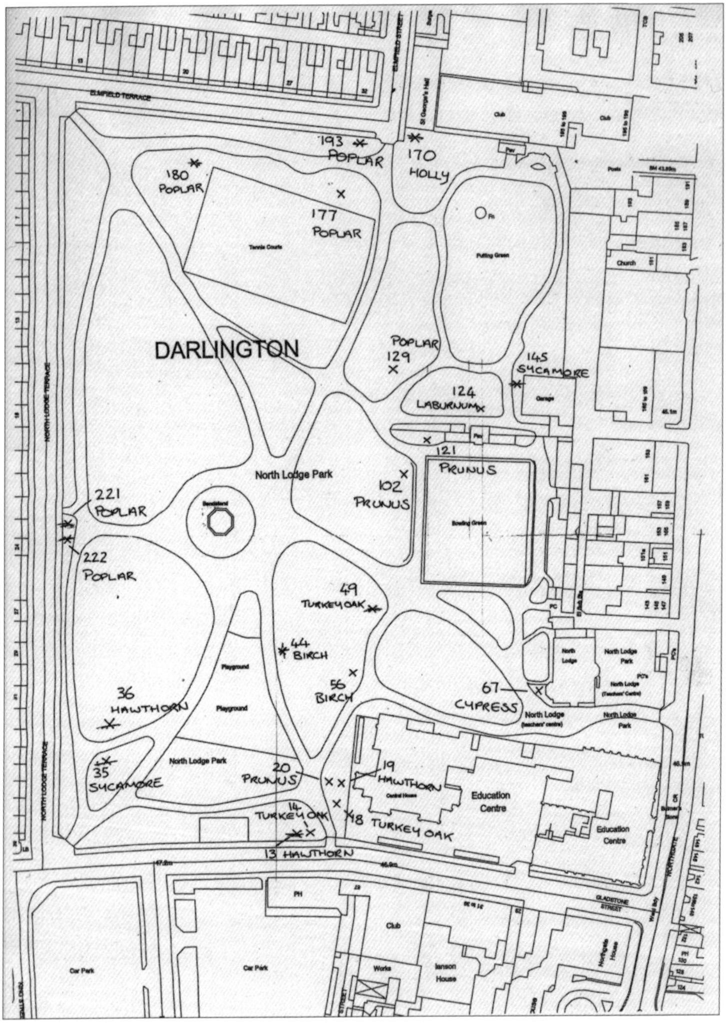
DARLINGTON
North Lodge Park
193 POPLAR
170 HOLLY
180 POPLAR
177 POPLAR
POPLAR 129
145 SYCAMORE
124 LABURNUM
121 PRUNUS
102 PRUNUS
221 POPLAR
222 POPLAR
49 TURKEY OAK
44 BIRCH
56 BIRCH
67 CYPRESS
36 HAWTHORN
35 SYCAMORE
20 PRUNUS
19 HAWTHORN
14 TURKEY OAK
18 TURKEY OAK
13 HAWTHORN
Tennis Courts
Putting Green
Bowling Green
Playground
Education Centre
ELMFIELD TERRACE
NORTH LODGE TERRACE
Club
Church
Garage
Car Park
GLADSTONE STREET
North Lodge Park

Where swaying crocuses
have bled together into a purple hue,
and spread like a cloak across the mound,
you squeeze past an old man
pushing his wife in a wheelchair
along a thin rocky path.

She hands him a white hankie
to wipe the sweat from his brow.
You wrap your scarf around your neck
to keep the cold out.

A young girl sits on the new bench,
three children squabble at her feet,
she rubs her rounded belly,
and lights up,
but her face is empty.
You move two seats down,
towards the nearest exit,

look at the ground.
A red-eyed, black-eyed blond
shuffles past; her anorak pulled tightly across her chest,
the weight of it, too much.

Love-stripped teenagers
ride aimlessly in circles.
You watch two grey squirrels
chasing round a poplar.

Bored boys throw stones
into a dried up fountain.
When they leave,
you check the damage,

imagine how there might have been
a bubbling over,
a playful trickle.

Cross words between mother and son
are hammered home like nails
as she drags him behind her.
You listen to a clacking magpie,

and remember The Assembly of God,
            the Luncheon Club,
where you heard stories about a frozen lake,
a white swan, a black swan,
about an air raid shelter,
railings for the war effort.
You miss the crown of dead flowers
near the bandstand.

You, the poet,
you're in your bedroom,
pulling notes together,
forming verse
            to honour life in the park.
You see a spider
hanging without fault
from the ceiling.
You bring it down with your poetry clipboard,
flush it away,
wash your hands.

Two Turkey Oaks

(Trees Number 14 and 18)

'If trees could scream, would we be so cavalier about cutting them down? We might, if they screamed all the time, for no good reason'
Jack Handley

You two!
standing guard,
North Lodge Park's own Gog and Magog.
You hold open a narrow gate to mystery.
Could you not foresee your own fate,
your days, ticking away
with each catkin pendulum sway.

Take a look at yourselves,
it's not new life that springs from you,
but cancers, stealing your thunder.
Face it, your feet are weary
as you head towards other dimensions,
a new world, different reality.

Yet still, you're laughing.
Is that because you don't understand,
or is it simply your male and female energies of nature;
the realisation that you've been fulfilled?
And does that mean,
when the cutter comes,
that we won't hear you scream?

Hawthorn

(Tree Number 19)

'If what I say resonates with you, it is merely
because we are both branches on the same tree.'
WB Yeats

According to Bose, the Indian Botanist,
we should be able to hear your heartbeat
and the sap rising like blood in your veins,
but there's nothing now.
This time your crown of thorns
is a sign of your own dying.

The stories of sorrow and joy
you listened to in your shade
as we stretched at your foot in peace,
will go with you to the grave.

We don't draw a line under you,
but make a circle, where you stood.
And in honour of your flowering,
no one will enter the ring
'til the turn of Spring.

Prunus

(Trees Number 20, 102 and 121)

'The wonder is that we can see these trees and not wonder more.'
Ralph Waldo Emerson

Purple leaves darken for the last time
No fingers stretch for the sun
No princess-weddings in the sky
No pink posies taken home
No flower-crowns for little girls,
Your five-petalled blossom days are done.

Sycamore

(Tree Number 35)

'God has cared for these trees, saved them from drought, disease, avalanches, and a thousand tempests and floods. But he cannot save them from fools.'
John Muir

I've heard people call you weed.
True enough, you seem content
to twirl your seed
and set down roots anywhere.

On this day of your measuring
we treat you with disdain
as we talk of how we'll cut you down to size,
how we'll dispose of your remains.

We show more interest
in the artist's fungus at your foot,
than how you feel
about loosing sight of the children.

Had I not been too proud,
I would have knelt down,
and with my fingernail,
gently carved my initials
in your ganoderma.

Hawthorn

(Tree Number 36)

'Give me a land of boughs in leaf,
A land of trees that stand;
Where trees are fallen there is grief;
I love no leafless land.'
AE Housman

Valerian of the Heart,
you're to be hedged out.
For all your love of man
you form the dividing line
between ruler and ruled.
Your door to the underworld
shows fiery feuds where prayers burn
before they can reach heaven.
Some liken you to Eris;
more blackthorn than rose.

But branches grow heavy this April.
Already there are enough snow-white petals
to make a bridal gown;
and she can't wait to dance around.
One twig protects her from stormy seas;
as she takes from you, the bread and cheese she needs.

She doesn't notice your rotting roots.
and in any case,
maybe a handkerchief tree,
planted in your place
will help to dry her tears.

Birch

(Tree Number 56)

'That tree whose leaves are trembling:
is yearning for something.
That tree so lovely to see, acts as if it wants to flower:
it is yearning for something.'
Diego Hurtado de Mendoza, 1395

So much for your new starts and beginnings reputation;
You've let yourself be crowded out.
You can be as delicate as you like,
shake your tracery of thin twigs and branches,
fact is you need space to do your fairy dance,
and you've lost it!

Never again will we sit under your little catkins
or watch the undersides of your leaves pinken.
Why didn't you dig deeper,
set your roots down further?

Your silver trunk no longer catches the moon.
This is the beginning of the end for you.

Cypress

(Tree Number 67)

'Today I have grown taller from walking with the trees.'
Karle Wilson Baker

Looking back, you weren't even on my list.
I picked out your name from a map of crosses;
appropriate really, given your role
            as the mourning tree.

And despite your hatred of loneliness,
the plan showed you as totally alone.
It was as if by isolating you
we could deny our own death.

Cyparissus, one little mistake put you here,
turned your arms into flattened twigs,
covered you with scale-like needles
made you cry.

Enough of this eternal grief
we will not use your hard wood for coffins
but carve instead, a stag from your remains.

Silver Birch

(Tree Number 44)

'I'd like to go by climbing a birch tree,
And climb black branches up a snow-white trunk
Toward heaven till the tree could bear no more,
But dipped its top and set me down again.
That would be good both going and coming back.
One could do worse than be a swinger of birches.'
Robert Frost

Lady of the Woods,
you move on the gentlest of winds.
Children have blossomed under your branches,
skimmed your white trunk, up to the witch's knots.

Every night for sixty years
your silvery bark has glimmered in the moonlight,
fairies have bathed in its reflection.
Your rods have beaten out the playground's boundary.
You have sugared the tongues of lovers,
charmed the cots of babies
and cast away their weakness.
You have warded off evil;
been womanly and constant.

On behalf of those who are about to take you down,
I'm asking you to purify yourself with tears;
you're dying back, make way for the new.
I'm asking you out of respect
so that anger won't rise in your whipping-twigs.
You will be taken whole, nothing will be left;
no hollow silver tubes,
no writing parchment
on which to scribe these last few words
            in your honour.

Turkey Oak

(Tree Number 49)

'A fool sees not the same tree that a wise man sees.'
William Blake, Proverbs of Hell, *1790*

Scarred by the weight your hazard beams carry,
you've grown for light,
gnarled,
bent back on yourself.

I touch your wood as a sign of respect
            and for luck;
bow to your ten-metre crown,
though I know it's slipping.
You've been sentenced;
and it's too early for an oak of fifty.

When I look at you, I think of Adonis,
how he, having been born of a tree,
gave humanity a core of woody strength
and the soul of heaven-seeking branches.

And because you'll make no more woolly cups
            for me to carry,
I'll grow old,
remembering how you stuck your neck out
in these dark days leading up to Christmas;
how you stood, proud till the last, your elbows out.

Two Poplars

(Trees Number 221 and 222)

'A society grows great when old men plant trees
whose shade they know they shall never sit in.'
Greek proverb

So you needed more space; but you two, you
over-reached yourselves, got too big for your roots.
You dangled your catkins like North Sea gold,
scattered our ground with your cast-offs.
According to you, your seeds were so special
that they had to be wrapped in cotton down.
You were the Mr and Mrs Poplar
we couldn't keep up with. You had to go.
That's why you were pollarded.
We're good at that; it's what we British do.
If anyone gets ideas above their station
we wound them past their point of decay,
wait until their decorative days are done
and watch, while they die, slowly, from the inside.

Laburnum

(Tree Number 124)

'Except during the nine months before he draws breath,
no man manages his affairs as well as a tree does.'
George Bernard Shaw

You die and lean
behind the bowling green,
your ornamental purpose, gone.

People talk with knowing nods,
point to your brown, downy pods;
mention the poison you're capable of.

They've forgotten your sun-bright days,
how you yellowed their pathways
satisfied their ebony ways.

It's as if the rest of us have no badness.

Sycamore

(Tree Number 145)

'I like trees because they seem more resigned to
the way they have to live than other things do.'
Willa Cather,* O Pioneers, *1913

Caught between a garage
            and a putting green;
(might just as well be
            a rock and a hard place),
you put on a veneer of not caring
while you plan next year's fruit on wings.

But I know,
as I hold my ear to your cavities,
that there won't be enough of you
to make a wooden spoon
let alone a violin.
So I touch you,
hoping to feel the vibrato
of your last notes.

Hornbeam

(Unnumbered)

'There is always music amongst the trees in the garden,
but our hearts must be very quiet to hear it.'
Minnie Aumonier

When I was a cool beauty
I cared for my looks,
kept myself in good condition,
tried to make life as comfortable as possible.
I dreamed of unusual lovers
            and kindness.

Maybe I was wrong.

Decay has set in.
I have a definite lean.
I'm moss-greened and embarrassed,
            it's entirely my own fault.
And though I'm unnumbered,
I have to go.
I'm not being egoistic,
it's a question of discipline;
I'm blocking a healthy beach.

Maybe this is too reasonable.

March will be my final fling.
I'll fill the days with catkins
            and hope
that my iron grain will move pianos to music
and not become wielding mallets,
or skittles to be repeatedly brought down.

Maybe I'm over-optimistic.

Holly

(Tree Number 170)

'Sensing us, the trees tremble in their sleep,
The living leaves recoil before our fires,
Baring to us war-charred and broken branches,
And seeing theirs, we for our own destruction weep.'
Kathleen Raine

Snuggled up against the bricks
and needing little light,
he-holly prickles reflect like mirrors.

Leathery spikes have conducted
a thousand lightning strikes around the park,
but the wise fire will soon be out,
with no sharp blade forged from its embers.

Without the holly's subtle planes,
how do we transform our prickly bits,
improve our reaction to the world,
            chill out?

Storms in North Lodge Park

(January, 2005)

'The tree that moves some to tears of joy is in the eyes
of others only a green thing that stands in the way.'
William Blake

Another one down, a lime,
a 'limey', sliced through before your time
by a deadly troop of gales.

Odd that death should spread its fingers
at St. George's gate, where soldiers once lingered
over soup and hot, sweet tea.

In your doubt
you accept with composure, what life dishes out,
open-mouthed; obediently.

Only now, when you're snapped and broken
do you show your true colours, the token
of your loyalty; an inner wood, red as blood.

I look down at you; the parts that are dead and dying;
at your limp limbs lying
lifeless on a prickly yew

and wonder if there's enough of your core left standing
to remind you of your being;
whether, through sacrifice, you'll blossom again.

Two Poplars

(Trees Number 177 and 129)

'For in the true nature of things, if we rightly consider, every tree is far more glorious than if it were made of gold and silver.'
Martin Luther

After all you've been through,
after you've stood and absorbed
almost a hundred years of fear,
provided a shield for everyone,
focussed us on the light;
after you've soothed our bruises
and helped us face the harsh realities of life -
this is how we repay you.
You, who in the land of sunsets,
made magic and hoped for regeneration,
must give up your crowns,
be taken down.

Would that the hero
who silvered the undersides of your leaves,
had purged this world of all its monsters
before he left.

Poplar

(Populis Niagra Italica - Tree Number 193)

'For the tree of the field is man's life'
Deuteronomy, 20:19

Each time you try to turn a new leaf
you're dealt the ace of spades.
Death is in the air,
yet even at this crossroads
you whisper incessantly.
It's your love of language
            that appeals to me.

You could shield yourself from the rot,
but you do not resist Hecate's will,
nor anoint yourself with scented balsam
to stop the bruising talk that will bring you down.
Instead, you face the ultimate sacrifice;
forgive them,
            aware that they know not what they do,
and quietly, by the railings of Elmfield Terrace,
you weep the bitter, amber tears of seven sisters.

Poplar

(Tree Number 180)

'What did the tree learn from the earth
to be able to talk with the sky?'
Pablo Neruda

Once you were in your element
in North Lodge air,
but this is your time cycle,
as you disappear into your own cavities.
You have lost your moon-magic,
you're shaking.

I'm going to think of you
as unsplintering floorboards,
or buoyant paddles;
your wood not stolen,
but given over gracefully,
as with fear absorbed,
you move, ever closer to the light.

Maureen Almond

Maureen Almond was born in Ferryhill, County Durham, in 1945; her childhood days were spent below the railway in Thornaby. She has a grown-up daughter and now lives in Yarm with her husband and dog. Maureen worked as a personnel manager before becoming a full-time writer and teacher. Writing residencies include BBC Radio Cleveland, Stockton online, St Luke's Hospital, Sunderland Education Action Zone, Newcastle Education Action Zone, and North Lodge Park, Darlington. She joined the editorial board of Mudfog Books in 2002.

As well as publication in numerous poetry magazines, she has published four other collections: *Hot* (Mudfog, 1997), *Tailor Tacks* (Mudfog, 1999), *Oyster Baby* (Biscuit, 2002) and *The Works* (Biscuit, 2004). She is currently working on her fifth collection.